simply

tarot

LEANNA GREENAWAY

A Sterling / Zambezi Book
Sterling Publishing Co., Inc.
New York

I would like to dedicate this book to my family, who have showed so much tolerance and patience during my hours of writing, and especially to Belita and John Greenaway for their help in compiling these pages.

Illustrations from the Rider-Waite Tarot Deck® reproduced by permission of
U.S. Games Systems, Inc., Stamford, CT 06902 USA.
Copyright © 1971 U.S. Games Systems, Inc.
Further reproduction prohibited.
The Rider-Waite Tarot Deck® is a registered trademark of U.S. Games Systems, Inc.

Library of Congress Cataloging-in-Publication Data Available

2   4   6   8   1 0   9   7   5   3   1

Published in 2005 by Sterling Publishing Co., Inc.
387 Park Avenue South, New York, NY 10016
Copyright © 2005 Leanna Greenaway
Illustrations Copyright © 2005 Hannah Firmin
Tarot spread illustrations by Robert Steimle
Published and distributed in the UK solely by Zambezi Publishing Limited
P.O. Box 221, Plymouth, Devon PL2 2YJ
Distributed in Canada by Sterling Publishing
c/o Canadian Manda Group, 165 Dufferin Street
Toronto, Ontario, Canada M6K 3H6
Distributed in Australia by Capricorn Link (Australia) Pty. Ltd.
P.O. Box 704, Windsor, NSW 2756, Australia

For information about custom editions, special sales, premium and
corporate purchases, please contact Sterling Special Sales
Department at 800-805-5489 or specialsales@sterlingpub.com.

Manufactured in China
All Rights Reserved

Zambezi ISBN 1 903065 46 1
Sterling ISBN 1-4027-2279-6

contents

1

THE FIRST STEPS ON THE ROAD

Tarot is a popular form of divination that people have been using for centuries. By following the guidelines set out in this book, you will come to understand how easy it is to master the art of reading cards. Many people complain that countless tarot books are contradictory or too difficult to follow—and with thousands of different interpretations in circulation—it is not hard to see why some people struggle. This book brings tarot into the twenty-first century, making the card meanings easy to understand and follow. For the moment, try to forget anything that you have already picked up from other manuals and focus on the meanings set out in these pages.

Although tarot is primarily traditional, I offer modern and up-to-date translations for all seventy-eight cards. Afterwards, you can adapt other people's interpretations where appropriate. Throughout the book, we will be grouping the cards together and working mainly with the Celtic Cross spread. To be successful in completing your knowledge, try not to skip through the book, but look at it more as a teaching manual, with each chapter taking you through the process of learning tarot.

Obviously, you will need a pack of tarot cards, preferably ones that you choose yourself. Be sure to obtain a relatively traditional deck that has full illustrations on all the cards rather than just a collection of Cups, Wands, Swords, and Pentacles. A tarot deck is comprised of seventy-eight cards: twenty-two major arcana cards and fifty-six minor arcana cards.

HOUSING

Housing the cards is important. Purchase a small wooden box and a length of silk. Each time you have finished with your cards, wrap them in the silk and pop them away safely in their box. Some readers like to familiarize themselves with their cards and frequently bring them out to shuffle them. Another tradition is to place them on the highest shelf in the house, as this is supposed to produce a more powerful influence. You could go one step farther and put them under your pillow at night. Choose your deck carefully, because even after many years of reading, you will always prefer to revert to using your old, faithful deck.

AM I PSYCHIC?

We have to go back to the beginning of time—to an age when man's main aim was to survive. The ancients relied on their instincts because without them they were vulnerable to danger. Many were so in tune with their natural instinct that they could predict things such as weather patterns and earthquakes. The Druids and pagans worshiped the land, studied moon phases, and became familiar with the seasons. This helped them to recognize the best time for planting and harvesting crops.

Unfortunately, man today seems swept away with the busy high-tech side of life. We are so consumed by technology and materialism that we have lost touch with our inner selves and the world around us. To become more psychic we need to go back to basics and fill some of our spare time with meditating and reading spiritually orientated literature.

When we compare our lifestyle to how our predecessors lived, we have without a doubt lost our way. We are finally starting to realize the powerful influence of our inherent abilities. We all maintain a certain degree of psychic ability, and with concentration and dedication, we can light up the spark that lies within us all.

Tarot is the key to unlocking the psyche. Like anything you want to achieve, the more you practice a subject, the better you become. If I were to start an apprenticeship in plastering walls, after time I would begin to master the art. It's the same with tarot: once you begin to understand how it works, after a while the cards will enhance your psychic flow and open your mind to a higher plane.

If you have suppressed your psychic flow, you can use the tarot to jump-start it and to guide you. Even the best clairvoyants do not wake up psychic every morning. Anything can cause our vibration to be blocked—a poor night's sleep, stress, or even too much concentration. Even if you are not a natural psychic, the tarot will always predict a situation, so your challenge is to learn how to interpret the cards in order to give a precise account of them. The tarot's accuracy is spectacular, and many skeptics eat their words after someone has given them a reading. Because of this, more people are finally accepting the tarot as part of everyday life and are consulting readers on a regular basis.

GENDER

I have used the female gender throughout this book. This is not because I am a bra-burning feminist but because more women than men learn the tarot and consult tarot readers, and also because it is a nice change.

HOW THE TAROT WORKS

Most tarot card readers believe in guides or guardian angels. These are our spirit companions who watch over us throughout our lifetime. There are two different types of guides. First, some believe that loved ones who have passed over will continue looking out for us and that they give comfort in times of stress. Second, there are the guides from the hierarchy. These spirits have reincarnated through many lifetimes in order to perfect their souls, making them capable and practical in guiding us through our life. They are known as the "divine beings," or spirit helpers, who visit our subconscious minds and bring messages via our dream sleep.

They appear as male or female, and they are expert in steering us through certain situations. Therefore, we may have more than one guide, as throughout our lives we face many different circumstances. Some people have been lucky enough to see or speak directly with their guardian angels. Mediums do this often because they can easily create the channel of communication. A medium opens her mind to receive messages from the other side, and the tarot does the same for those who learn to read it. The reader must interpret what the cards say and then communicate the message to the client. In many cases, some readers feel an urge to say something that is not apparent in the cards. Some use the term "vision," but it is mostly a strong feeling that the reader experiences which relates to the person for whom they are reading.

When we open ourselves to being psychic, we cannot really take the credit for the information that we relay. Without our guides assisting us, we would not be able to correspond at all. By opening our vibration, we become like a telephone line. One can describe it as being similar to tuning in to a radio station. If you are mediumistic, it may take a while before the voice is clear enough to hear. If you are anything like me, you won't hear the voice of your guide speaking to you at all. This is because, for some of us, they communicate only through our subconscious, making us feel confident in our predictions. Sometimes you may just say the first thing that springs into your head, and lo and behold, you astound your client with your accuracy. Guides work beautifully with the tarot, warning or foretelling of future happenings and giving advice through the cards. When a person shuffles the tarot, they are not aware of the fact that they are transporting their vibration on to the cards. It is also vital to encourage clients to shuffle the cards for a good two to three minutes and to concentrate on their problems while doing so. This will push the unseen energies into the cards, thus making them easy to read.

A FEW TIPS TO HELP YOU ALONG THE WAY

1. Throughout this book, I refer to the person you are reading for as the querent or the client.

2. Only read for the same person once in three months. Too many readings may confuse the querent.

3. Never allow someone else to conduct a reading with your cards. Only you can use your deck.

4. Never read for anyone if you are ill or upset. The reading may be thwarted and result in inaccuracy.

5. Even if the querent's cards look dismal or they are extremely depressed, try to emphasize the positive, because when a person is in a healthy frame of mind, she finds it easier to undertake complicated matters.

6. Don't make things up. Always say what you see. If something negative arises in a spread, follow it up with something positive, and give helpful advice on how to tackle the issues.

7. When performing a reading, have a source of salt nearby, or light a candle. If you decide to become professional and to read the tarot for strangers, a colorful mix of individuals will visit you. The salt and candles will help to protect you and keep your area cleansed.

8. If you are a woman, never read for a man if you are alone in the house. All strange men pose a threat to women, and it is imperative that you safeguard yourself. Every clairvoyant I have met has some tale to tell regarding a male client. Remember, in normal circumstances, you wouldn't let a strange man into your home without someone else being there. However confident you feel, do not assume that just because you have read for a man ten times, he won't pounce or become aggressive. (Apologies to all the nice men in the world, but we women must be cautious.)

9. Most people who visit you will have problems, and some desperate people come to tarot readers as a last resort. Many find comfort in a reading and use it as a crutch to keep going through problematic times. Always keep a list of useful phone numbers on your table. With the best will in the world, you will not be able to help everyone, and sometimes counselors who are specialized in certain fields can make all the difference.

10. It is always a good idea to get an answering machine. Clients will telephone you at all hours wanting to follow up on their reading or inform you if something predicted has occurred, and you will have no private life if you don't allow your answering machine to take these calls.

UPRIGHT AND REVERSED CARDS

The majority of tarot readers use the cards only in the upright position, but sometimes a card accidentally lands in the reversed position. When this happens, there is usually a good reason for it. I don't go into great detail in this book about reversed meanings, but I do give brief "reversed" interpretations for all the cards.

In some cases, it is worth looking at both the upright and the reversed interpretation, as this shows both sides of a person or a situation—and often that is what is wanted.

THE HISTORY AND ORIGINS OF THE TAROT

Nobody knows the origin of tarot, and there is much mystery surrounding where it originated. In the eighteenth century, Egyptology fascinated many people, so they believed that the tarot began its life in Egypt. We know from historical records that people used the tarot in the Renaissance period. A deck of tarot that dated back to the 1400s was found in Milan in Northern Italy. The pack was painted for the Visconti family and was later reproduced under the name "Visconti Tarocchi." However, the surviving decks were commonly French designs, and it was then thought that the tarot had been imported to Italy from France. If you would like to know more about the history of the tarot, read *Tarot Mysteries* by historian and tarot reader Jonathan Dee.

Tarot has changed considerably over the centuries. Many of the earlier decks were very basic; now they are far more detailed, making the pictures more inspirational to the reader. Cards were adapted to avoid associations with the Catholic religion, changing "the Pope" to "the Hierophant" or "the High Priest" and "the Papess" to "the High Priestess." In addition, the order in which the cards are placed has been modified throughout time. For instance, the Fool, which is traditionally the first card, is numbered 0 and originally sat at the end of the major arcana, making it card number 22. This occurred with many of the adaptations of tarot. There are thousands of different decks in circulation, so some interpretations will have been adjusted differently from others.

Tarot is more popular now than ever and is used on a far wider scale, thus making it interesting to people from all walks of life. Initially, many used the tarot as a card game, but it has also held a mystical and supernatural atmosphere for centuries. It was once felt that only a few privileged individuals possessed the gift to read tarot, but this is untrue. We all possess the ability to tune into our psyche and we are all capable of foretelling the future. While some people are born with psychic ability, others can learn to develop it. Every one of us is born with a sixth sense, and we all possess the power to tap in to our subconscious and coordinate it.

SOME BASIC CARD FACTS

There are seventy-eight cards in a deck of tarot.

Twenty-two are major arcana cards and fifty-six are minor arcana cards.

All twos in tarot represent choices and decisions.

All fives are generally bad news.

All eights symbolize good luck.

All pages represent children from birth to fifteen, and these can be either male or female.

Knights represent young men between ages fifteen and twenty-nine.

All queens represent ages above mature teenage girls.

All kings represent males over age thirty.

The word "reversed" is used to describe a card that is presented upside down.

THE COURT CARDS

The Court cards are the kings, queens, knights, and pages, and they are the trickiest cards to understand. Each has its own personality, hair, and eye coloring, and each has its hang-ups. Some students find the Court cards very hard to assess in a spread, because these cards do not always represent people. They can also signify situations.

AGE RANGES

- Kings are men age twenty-nine and over.

- Queens are ages above mature teenage girls.

- Knights are young men between ages seventeen and twenty-nine.

- Pages are male or female children from birth to fifteen years of age.

COLORING

The ideas here are traditional, so you can make use of them if you wish or you can go by the character of the Court card rather than any specific hair, eye, or skin color.

- CUPS blue to hazel eyes, light to brown hair

- WANDS blue-green eyes, fair skin, fair to red hair

- SWORDS dark eyes, dark hair, olive or black skin

- PENTACLES any color eyes, brown or black hair

If I do two spreads for the querent and the focus of the reading is her husband, he may appear as one king in one spread and another in the next. The first Court card might symbolize the person, while the second indicates the outcome of the situation, perhaps the way that the husband is changing or the way that the partnership is evolving.

SIGNIFICATORS

Before you start a reading, you can select a Court card that you feel resembles your client. This card becomes the significator. You can read cards without selecting a significator, but then you have to work out whether a card that appears in the spread relates to your client or not. For example, say you are reading for a thirty-three-year-old blue-eyed woman and the Queen of Swords appeared in the spread. This would alert you to the fact that this is not the querent, because this queen is traditionally dark-haired and dark-eyed.

In this situation, you must tune in to the tarot and look at the surrounding cards to establish a story. If there is no apparent link between the Court card and the querent, it is probable that the card refers to a forthcoming situation.

A CLEVER TIP

Where the Court cards are concerned, look at both the upright and reversed meanings, as even the nicest person can have an occasional off day and behave badly, while a nasty person can be lovely when in the right frame of mind.

EQUIVALENTS

Cups

- cauldrons in some decks

- hearts

- the water sign

- influenced by spring

- emotions, relationships, friends, and marriages

Wands

- batons, staffs, and wands in some decks

- clubs

- the fire sign

- influenced by summer

- work, ambitions, business, and property

Swords

- spades

- the air sign

- influenced by autumn

- health, medical issues, emotions, and relationship difficulties

Pentacles

- coins or discs in some decks

- diamonds

- the earth sign

- influenced by winter

- money, cash flow, business, property, and tuition

BIRTH SIGNS AND TIMINGS

Twelve of the major arcana cards have a birth sign attached to them. It is important that you learn these, as it is the only way you will be able to add timings to your readings. The predictions that you make will usually take around six to twelve months to come about, so using the birth signs helps you to pinpoint a time.

The Emperor

Aries = March/April

The High Priest/Hierophant

Taurus = April/May

The Lovers

Gemini = May/June

The Chariot

Cancer = June/July

Strength

Leo = July/August

The Hermit

Virgo = August/September

Justice

Libra = September/October

Death

Scorpio = October/November

Temperance

Sagittarius = November/December

The Devil

Capricorn = December/January

The Star

Aquarius = January/February

The Moon

Pisces = February/March

2

THE MAJOR ARCANA

The major arcana cards are the first twenty-two cards in a conventional deck of the tarot. Many people believe them to be much older than the minor arcana, but there is little evidence for this—although individual images may have been around before in some other form, after which they became incorporated into the tarot.

The images on the cards are extremely powerful, and many of them offer spiritual insight to a reading. It is important to learn the meaning of these cards thoroughly, as only then can you tap into the mystery of the cards to conduct an accurate reading.

THE FOOL.

THE FOOL
Card number 0 or 22

Traditional Points About the Card

The young person represented in this card is sometimes known as the Jester. He holds the white rose of innocence, which symbolizes everlasting life. In his hand he carries a package connected to a pole. Inside are the ingredients of life, given to him by God to do with as he likes. A small white dog is usually present on the card, accompanying him through his life. Fate and destiny rule both the man and the dog. This youth is generally unaware of life's dangers.

Modern Meaning

This is quite a positive card. The card is numbered 0, which indicates a moment in time before something is about to happen—if you like, a waiting time before embarking on a new adventure. This is a starting point in the querent's life. A new path awaits her, but she must be patient, as there are likely to be delays. Tell the querent she must prepare herself to take a different direction in life but not to jump in with both feet. She should stop and listen to her instincts before rushing ahead. For a time the querent will feel insecure, and, because of this, she will find herself being thoughtless or insensitive. To see what the new path is, look at the surrounding cards in the spread. It may be a new job or relationship that is approaching or even recovery after ill health.

Reversed

The querent will constantly feel as if she is stuck in a rut and never moving on. She will go through a spell of being selfish and unpopular.

Key Points

- a new path awaits the querent
- an insecure time
- look before you leap
- being thoughtless or insensitive

THE MAGICIAN.

THE MAGICIAN
Card number 1

Traditional Points About the Card

Throughout time, the Magician has also been referred to as "the Juggler" or "the Showman." His name in the beginning was "Magus," meaning magician. The card shows him standing in front of a table wearing a red cloak. On the table are various representations of the four suits of tarot. His right hand holds the scroll of knowledge and he points to the heavens. His left hand, which is said to be the hand of healing, points downward. Around his waist, a snake eats its own tail, demonstrating neverending life. The symbol above his head, which looks like a figure eight on its side, is called a "nimbus," and this brings spiritual protection.

Modern Meaning

This card carries divine occult protection. Always tell the querent that she is protected by a higher being. The querent must take a bold step forward in life, using and trusting her instincts. Everything is possible when God's love is present. This is also a psychic card, so advise her to start the process of developing her psychic abilities. This can be done through meditation. Willpower and determination is needed to get through life's hard lessons, but if the querent has faith in God, the divine being will place his hand in hers. Even if the querent does not feel as if she is going down the right path, reassure her that she is.

Reversed

The querent may send out negative thoughts, and she must be careful that she does not attract bad luck. She will not apply herself in the correct way, and she must change her attitude in order to succeed. Deceit and lies will be present in her life, so inform her to create harmony wherever she can.

Key Points

- the querent must use willpower to create harmony
- take a bold step forward
- use and develop psychic abilities

THE HIGH PRIESTESS
Card number 2

Traditional Points About the Card

This card symbolizes a female guide. Sometime decks call the High Priestess "Juno" or "the Female Pope." This is an exceptionally spiritual card. The scroll that she grasps contains all the secrets of life, because the knowledge is hers. Behind the veil, you can see water, and this represents the knowledge of spirit. She is the female version of the Magician.

THE HIGH PRIESTESS.

Modern Meaning

She is the lady guide, sometimes referred to as the mother or grandmother figure in spirit. If the querent has no such relative in spirit, then a high female guide will watch and protect her. The High Priestess is usually present in a person's reading if things are a little uncertain. She brings balance, promising that the fate of the querent is in the hands of the spirit world. The card itself is really lucky. Good things will appear in time, so the querent should be patient and refuse to listen too much to others, because they may be wrong. Encourage the querent to go with her feelings in all matters.

Reversed

If this card sits next to health cards, a family member might become ill. The querent should not trust others blindly. The querent will lack stamina, which indirectly could affect a relationship. Support will be needed.

Key Points

- the mother or grandmother in spirit
- divine spiritual protection
- things take off soon
- be patient

THE EMPRESS
Card number 3

Traditional Points About the Card

This is the fertility card, which shows growth in all things. The growth might apply to business, love, marriage, children, and much else. The Empress sits on a throne surrounded by the fruits of the harvest, representing fruitfulness. In some decks, there is a bird in a cage. Some call the Empress a Mother Earth figure. The throne, shield, and scepter demonstrate maternal power. Look closely at her hair, because in some decks you will see a head-dress showing the constellations of the zodiac.

Modern Meaning

If this card appears in a reading, it usually represents the maternal figure in the family.

If you are reading for a woman of childbearing age, it could indicate a future pregnancy. Regarding pregnancy, if the querent is past childbearing age, then there may be news of a pregnancy within the family. With a young female, this could warn of a pregnancy, which she may or may not want. If the Empress appears in a man's cards, a partner, daughter, or some other family member will be embarking on motherhood.

You need to look at surrounding cards to establish who might be getting pregnant. It may have nothing to do with pregnancy, though; it may simply show that the querent is a solid maternal figure who takes her responsibilities toward her family very seriously.

If there are three or more Sword cards present in the same spread as the Empress, the querent or someone around her might find it difficult to conceive.

Reversed

The querent or someone close to her may have conception problems. This card in the reversed position can indicate complacency and taking things for granted.

Key Points

- a pregnancy to come for the family
- a maternal figure
- fulfillment and fruitfulness in some area of life

THE EMPEROR
Card number 4

Birth Sign

Aries

Traditional Points About the Card

The Emperor is the father figure, and tarot readers see him as being in control. Sometimes stern and very materialistic, he holds a position of authority, demanding respect from those around him. The Emperor is not easy to influence, and he will always follow his own judgment. Quite Victorian in his approach, he speaks his mind. Being so matter-of-fact and occasionally judgmental can sometimes make him unpopular. In his eyes, his duty is to protect all that is his.

Modern Meaning

This man could hold the Aries birth sign. Alternatively, events shown in the reading could happen around March and April. This is also a business card, so if you have several wands in the spread, it would be fair to suggest that the reading is work-related. Legal dealings may arise for the querent, particularly if the Justice card is also present.

Reversed

The querent will feel the weight of family responsibility. She will start projects and then find that she is unable to finish them. She might have a thief involved in her life.

Key Points

- Aries for timing
- a boss, father figure, or authority figure
- legal or business dealings

THE HIEROPHANT.

THE HIEROPHANT
Card number 5

Birth Sign

Taurus

Traditional Points About the Card

The Hierophant is perceived as God's right-hand man, sometimes known as "the High Priest" or "the Pope," thus making this card extremely spiritual. He holds a staff of office in his left hand, which transmits to the earth's power. His right hand rests in the blessing position. He sits before the keys of the Vatican, which will unlock the knowledge of God.

Modern Meaning

This is one of the most spiritual cards of all seventy-eight. This high male guide looks down over the querent throughout the journey of life. He protects marriage and family matters and steps in to ease burdens. Delays are highly featured in the querent's life, so encourage her to be patient and tell her that her guide will work for her benefit. Also, tell her to focus on spiritual matters rather than material ones, as this will help her spirit to evolve faster. The keys on the card indicate a house move, and this prediction very often works.

Use Taurus for timing events.

Reversed

The querent must not be afraid to undertake a new project. She should explore every avenue with an open mind.

Key Points

- a high male guide in the spirit world
- focus on the spiritual rather than the material
- a house move
- Taurus for timing

THE LOVERS.

THE LOVERS

Card number 6

Birth Sign

Gemini

Traditional Points About the Card

This card corresponds to the traditional Romeo and Juliet story, and the lilies on the card represent a phallic symbol.

Modern Meaning

The divinatory meaning of the Lovers card varies depending on the circumstances, but in some ways, the card's title says it all. The Lovers means love affairs, relationships, and sexual attraction.

If the Lovers card is present in the same spread as any of the marriage cards, the couple will have a loving, stimulating relationship. If you establish that the querent is married or with a partner, and the Lovers falls in the same spread with any of the following cards—the Devil, the Two of Swords, the Three of Swords, or the Five of Pentacles, the opportunity for an affair will arise. However, what happens next is always the querent's decision.

When you are dealing with relationships of this kind in tarot, never confidently predict that the client will have an affair. It comes down to her free will in the end. She may have a Brad Pitt look-alike chasing her, but the test comes when she has to face facts and ask herself whether her present relationship is worth losing. Even if you have recognized that the querent is terribly unhappy in her relationship, do not assume that she will run into the arms of a wonderful lover. Many women whose partners beat, abuse, and neglect them stay with their partners regardless.

If you come to read the cards professionally in the future, you will discover that this situation is very common. Most married people will have temptation thrown in their path at some point in their life. Some will eat the forbidden fruit; others will not. Fate often tests the strongest of relationships. You may come across a married woman who is idyllically happy, but it does not mean that temptation will not test her. If the querent is already involved in a love triangle, look at the surrounding cards to see the outcome. You may see divorce, remarriage, or any number of other scenarios.

If she is single, she will embark on a relationship within the next twelve months.

Reversed

There will be fighting and arguing in a relationship.

Key Points

- the possibility of a love affair
- if the client is single, an impending new relationship
- Gemini for timing

Let us say that you see the husband being unfaithful to the querent; in a situation like this you have to tread very carefully. You may be wrong, so it is best to warn the client that she might hear news of someone around her having an affair. Even if she suspects that her partner is cheating, never stick your neck out and say that he is. He may not be. If you tape your reading, he could listen to it and come hammering on your door. Be sure to safeguard yourself in every instance.

THE CHARIOT
Card number 7

Birth Sign

Cancer

Traditional Points About the Card

The charioteer is ·said to be the son of the Empress and the Emperor. His strength comes from his father and his spiritual blessings from his mother. His task is to steer the chariot on its path through life, being cautious while controlling the horses in addition to controlling himself. There is one black horse and one white horse. Black signifies bad and white good, so the charioteer can decide whether he wants to be good or bad. The decision is his.

Modern Meaning

This card means travel, so imagine the charioteer upon his carriage as a form of transport. Although it is often interpreted as a journey, it is unlikely to be overseas; it is more likely to be a trip by automobile in the querent's own country. Being anything from a two-week vacation to a business meeting, the travel time will be short. This is also the card of movement, which denotes that the querent will be able to put her plans into action and can expect things to happen suddenly. Advise her that she is in control of her time and that she must not let her life descend into chaos.

If any relationship or family cards are in the spread, quarrels and arguments lie ahead. If the querent is a man, he should control his sexual urges.

Use Cancer for timing.

Reversed

Nothing will happen for a while. Plans and changes are on hold. Expect delays in travel. Problems with an automobile will cost money the querent can ill afford.

Key Points

- travel in one's own country
- choices between good and bad
- quarrels and rows between family members
- movement and change
- Cancer for timing

STRENGTH
Card number 8

Birth Sign

Leo

Traditional Points About the Card

This was once seen as being a merciless card, but over time its meaning has been toned down. This card represents man's dominion over the animal kingdom and reminds us that we should love and treat all animals with the respect that they deserve. The white robe denotes strength and purity.

Modern Meaning

This card shows that the querent must use her strength; it may refer to physical strength if she is recovering from an illness or emotional strength if she is experiencing problems. Encourage her to give to others and to show her inner qualities of love, patience, and gentleness. Although things could be tough for a while, tell her never to give up. If she uses her strength in a positive way, all things will work out well in the end. The obstacles she encounters may not be as bad as they first seem, so tell the querent to look for solutions, face issues, and not walk away.

If the Strength card is next to family cards, then your client may be thinking of acquiring a pet.

Reversed

Someone is being cruel to animals or people. The querent gives in to basic harsh instincts. Abuse is apparent in a relationship or unfaithfulness is evident in a marriage.

Key Points

- use strength in all areas of life
- look for solutions to problems
- never give up
- Leo for timing

THE HERMIT

Card number 9

Birth Sign

Virgo

Traditional Points About the Card

This is the guiding card of wisdom and truth. The lantern pictured in most decks guides the way. This is not a materialistic card but one that demonstrates peace and harmony and improving on the imperfections of the soul. The Hermit will help the questioner to develop spiritually.

THE HERMIT.

Modern Meaning

This card represents high spiritual protection. Someone in the spirit world is looking out for the querent. This could be a guardian angel or a father or grandfather figure. Usually this card appears when the querent is going through a particularly rough time. In rare circumstances, if many negative or disruptive cards are in the spread, she may be feeling suicidal—or someone close to her could be. The querent will go through a forlorn or depressed stage, searching for companionship or for a purpose in life. Tell her to take some quiet time out to reflect on her life.

Reversed

The querent will refuse to see what is available to her. She is burying her head in the sand. She has little faith and is spiritually isolated or unaware of the spiritual side of life. She might be the type who always puts herself before others.

Key Points

- father or grandfather figure in spirit
- feeling down or searching for a purpose in life
- take some time out
- Virgo for timing

THE WHEEL OF FORTUNE
Card number 10

WHEEL of FORTUNE.

Traditional Points About the Card

In some decks, we see a man and a woman celebrating. They are king and queen of all they have. Usually dressed in purple, they represent wisdom, spiritual matters, and royalty. The card itself indicates the wheel of the year and the circle of life. The end is the beginning, and life is everlasting.

Modern Meaning

Many readers see this as a bad card, perceiving that life's lessons may be hard. When one problem is solved, another surfaces, but life is very much like that anyway. Because of life's cruel blows, the querent might feel sorry for herself, so persuade her to understand that the world is like a big school. The lessons that she goes through are part of the spiritual plan that speeds her evolution to a higher plane of spirituality.

If you have a wealthy querent or someone who has plenty of money, she must not focus so much on the materialistic side of life. Tell her that God can take away as quickly as he gives—therefore, she must not take her monetary fortune for granted.

Have you ever heard the expression "What goes around comes around"? The law of karma is all-important, so always be grateful for what you have.

This card can suggest that things are going around in circles for a while.

Reversed

Advise the querent not to take chances with her health. The querent is run-down or depressed.

Key Points

- what goes around comes around
- going round in circles and not getting anywhere
- the querent must face life's hard lessons

JUSTICE
Card number 11

Birth Sign

Libra

Traditional Points About the Card

Justice shows a woman holding scales in her left hand. With her right hand, she holds a double-edged sword.

Modern Meaning

This is the legal card. Normally if this comes into a reading, it implies legal dealings of some kind. Therefore, this can indicate the need to consult a lawyer, to give evidence in court, move house, make an insurance claim, or cope with something similar. It can even revolve around something commonplace but irritating, such as a parking or speeding fine. Look at the cards close by to conclude the outcome of the situation.

Justice can also imply karmic payback time, so the querent's life should be kept balanced and in order. She must be honest in all she does. If she is trying to fool those around her, eventually they will suspect that something is wrong. People might try to influence the querent, so she must stick to her guns.

The scales are a good representation of the sign of Libra.

Reversed

The querent will be around police involvement, crime, or criminal activities.

Key Points

- a legal card
- things must stay in balance
- the querent should not try to fool others, because they will begin to suspect
- Libra for timing

THE HANGED MAN.

THE HANGED MAN
Card number 12

Traditional Points About the Card

This card shows a man hanging by his foot from a branch with his hands behind his back. His legs are crossed in acknowledgment to God. The two trees epitomize choices. Money falls from the man's pockets, implying that he is in danger of losing what he needs to survive.

Modern Meaning

When we look closely at this card, it shows that the querent has very little control over her life. She is waiting or hanging around and anticipating the future. It is important that the querent take a step back from reality and try to meditate to change her point of view. This is also the card of change, but although things may be slow or in limbo now, within a twelve-month period things will change. An easier way to remember this meaning is that the querent could be hanging around for up to a year, waiting for the changes to come about.

Reversed

Trust in God and absorb earthly feelings. Be cautious with do-gooders or someone who makes empty promises.

Key Points

- hanging around waiting for change
- big things to happen within one year
- meditation is needed

DEATH
Card number 13

Birth Sign

Scorpio

Traditional Points About the Card

On the card is a white rose, symbolizing purity and innocence. Death as we know it does not exist: life is a continuing cycle of existence—birth . . . death . . . birth . . . death. Through life's lessons, reincarnation teaches us to evolve on to a higher level.

Modern Meaning

Before we start, this card does not symbolize death as a reality in the context of someone dying. The Death card represents the end of one chapter in life and the beginning of another. This is also the card of change—off with the old and on with the new. Nowadays when this card appears in a spread, it actually registers positive news in most readings. Traditionally death only predicts an actual death around the querent when it is with the Nine or Ten of Swords. Let's face it; few of us go through a year without hearing that someone we know has passed over.

This is a card of rebirth and fresh beginnings. It can point toward the birth of a child if it is close by pregnancy cards such as the Empress. It could suggest the offer of a new job if it is sitting next to the Ace of Wands.

Many people shy away from the Death card, thinking it will predict the end of someone's life. Look at it as the end of an era and inform the querent not to be anxious if it appears in a reading.

Use Scorpio for timing.

Reversed

Total panic and disruption will be around the querent's life. Inform her that there is a light at the end of the tunnel and that she should keep battling on.

Key Points

- changes
- the beginning of a new era
- a birth
- death for someone around the querent, if it appears with the Nine or Ten of Swords

Dealing with Death in a Reading

Many clients panic about this card appearing in their reading, and in most decks, even the look of the card can be quite ghastly and unpleasant. It is very important when you are conducting a reading to approach the subject of death sensitively. You may not know the person you are reading for, so you will not be able to judge her reaction.

When reading tarot, I always try to encourage the "say what you see" approach but inexperienced or insensitive readers can instill fear into their clients by predicting a death. It is actually quite rare to see death in the cards, even though we will all have to experience grief in our lives at some point. However, in the developed world in the present era, death is not commonplace, so do not be too confident in predicting it. When approaching this subject, follow the guidelines listed below to make the querent feel more at ease.

1. Look at nearby cards. There may not be any grief or misery in the spread, thus suggesting that changes are more likely than losing someone.

2. If you feel a death is imminent, tell the client that they will hear news of a death rather than indicating that they will experience one at first hand.

3. Suggest instead that the querent may have to put a comforting arm around the shoulder of a friend.

4. Suggest that the querent will have an opportunity to pay respects to someone who has passed away but without shedding any tears. This way the death does not play on the client's mind. Should the querent go on to lose someone dear to her, she will appreciate your honesty in bringing the matter out in the reading—even though you do not "have it quite right."

5. Never say the words "I can see a death in the cards" because you might implant the idea that someone the querent loves will die. Believe me; some people's imaginations can run wild!

6. Never assume there will be a death or feel confident enough to predict this. You are not God, and you may be wrong.

7. If you are uncertain, say nothing at all; just indicate that this card means that a particular situation is ending and that it will make way for a new one. In a way, then, the Death card says what it means: that is, that something will die away in order for something new to come in.

If you go on to be a professional reader, you will find that most of the people who come to see you will be in the middle of some dilemma. Their lives are likely to be upside down or particularly difficult at that time. Although it is important to read the cards in a divinatory fashion, it is equally important not to send the querent away feeling worse than when she arrived. If you do this, then you have failed as a reader.

Death is a funny issue. Everyone deals with it differently. Some clients may be nervous or uneasy, and this can distort the reading in their mind. Always play the idea of actual death down and send the querent away with hope in her heart.

TEMPERANCE
Card number 14

Birth Sign

Sagittarius

Traditional Points About the Card

Sagittarius is the prophet of knowledge. On many cards, an angel is usually seen pouring water from one cup to another. The water is a cleansing agent. The angel has one foot on land and one foot in the water, portraying balance and harmony.

Modern Meaning

The guardian angel illustrated on this card is the querent's guide. Reassure her that this spirit is protecting her and looking after her at all times. Destiny has a hand in everything she does, so even if things are not as clear as she would like them to be, in time answers will come. Temperance also represents patience, self-control, and discipline. The individual's moods may be unbalanced, so tell her to think about those around her and to weigh up situations carefully.

Use Sagittarius for timing.

Reversed

Emotional frustration will cause stress. This is not the right time to begin new projects. The querent shouldn't waste her time by trying to do the impossible. A conflict in business leaves the querent searching for changes.

Key Points

- the guardian angel is watching
- weighing up two situations
- patience
- Sagittarius for timing

THE DEVIL
Card number 15

Birth Sign

Capricorn

Traditional Points About the Card

The man and woman on the card are bound to the devil due to their weakness. The devil thrives on man's imperfections and feeds off negative energies.

Modern Meaning

This is quite a complicated card and not a particularly nice one. In some decks, this card is called "Temptation"; hence the idea of weakness or lust. Greed or perversion is not always the case, but the card can point toward the fact that the querent will be in contact with someone who is cunning.

Relationships or marital affairs could face problems, and in some cases, they might end. If this card lies close to a number of Swords, there may be violence in a partnership or, at the very least, verbal abuse. If the Lovers card is in close proximity, sexual perversions or an element of kinkiness could be evident in a relationship, although I doubt that any reader would ever have the guts to come out and say it! If this card is close to a relationship card, it is doubtful that the affair is a healthy one.

There can be health issues here in connection with the head or with mental illness. I have also heard of it indicating skin diseases or something that causes itching, connected with the idea of burning in hell!

Use Capricorn for timing.

Reversed

An exceptionally bad character lurks around the individual. Danger is near, so tell the querent to ask for spiritual protection.

Key Points

- greed, perversion, and lust
- being around someone who isn't very nice
- poor health relating to the head, mental illness, or the skin
- capricorn for timing

THE TOWER
Card number 16

THE TOWER.

Traditional Points About the Card

Lightning is striking the Tower, and dirty water lies around its base. The Tower card shows two people falling helplessly from it. They are undoubtedly falling from grace.

Modern Meaning

As you can see, this is quite a disruptive card. Things in the querent's life could become difficult, and there will be many obstacles ahead. This can relate to breakups in relationships and friendships, alongside arguments, fights, and quarrels. To forgive is hard, but try to encourage the querent to see things from a different perspective. Changes will come along and bring about a new awareness. Sometimes the querent may be in for a spate of ill health, or she may hear of an accident.

Reversed

Head injuries or accidents are possible, as are depression and disaster.

Key Points

- breakups in relationships and friendships
- accidents and poor health
- quarrels and arguments

THE STAR.

THE STAR
Card number 17

Birth Sign

Aquarius

Traditional Points About the Card

The card shows an unclothed maiden with two ewers of water; this describes giving and receiving gifts. Her state of undress shows us that she has no need for material wealth.

Modern Meaning

This is the highest, most spiritual card of all. The Star represents guidance from above—the kind that is more powerful than any other kind. If the Tower is next to the Star, the querent's spiritual guides will protect her from anything bad, but she must meditate and try to understand a spiritual faith in more depth. This is also the humanitarian card, meaning that the querent will help others by giving them hope and inspiration. Wishes and dreams will be fulfilled in time.

Use Aquarius for timing.

Reversed

The person will show a lack of faith, but she has no need to worry.

Key Points

- highest card of protection
- this is humanitarian card, so the querent should help others
- Aquarius for timing

THE MOON
Card number 18

Birth Sign

Pisces

Traditional Points About the Card

This card, by tradition, shows a moon shining between two towers. One tower is good, indicating spiritual growth and development, and the other is unpleasant, representing material greed. A crayfish is crawling from the water, which could nip at the querent's feet unexpectedly.

Modern Meaning

Things are not as they seem. In some decks, this is called the card of illusion. Look deeper for undercurrents and deceit. The querent must listen and trust her instincts, for she will be right in the end. Situations around the querent may not be open and obvious, or someone close could be concealing a secret. Advise her not to be too trusting and to look closely at what others are doing so that they do not

55

take her in by lying to her. The individual needs to be cautious of idle gossip and must not believe everything she hears.

If the querent is female, and if there are health cards in the spread, she may encounter some gynecological problems. For a male, there may be stomach ulcers.

Use Pisces for timing.

Reversed

A mystery will be solved after a long wait. The querent should beware of secret enemies.

THE SUN.

Key Points

- lies and deceit
- secrets surround the client
- for a female, gynecological problems
- for a male, stomach ulcers
- Pisces for timing

THE SUN
Card number 19

Traditional Points About the Card

The powerful rays shine down on all.

Modern Meaning

This is unquestionably the best card in tarot, followed closely by the Ace of Cups as a predictor of good things. Whatever is happening in the querent's life, and no matter what obstacles she faces, the outcome will be a happy one.

If the Sun is in the same spread as a relationship card, romance will thrive. If it is around cards of health, then a full recovery can be expected. If the Sun is near cards that indicate poverty or money problems, extra cash will come in. This truly wonderful card promises that all things will work out well in the end.

Tip

It is rare to see the Ace of Cups in the same spread as the Sun, but should you see this, everything will be magnificent, and the querent should expect amazingly good fortune.

Reversed

There could be a risk of fire, but this will not result in anything too serious.

Key Points

- totally positive in every way
- things improving
- the best card in the deck
- with the Ace of Cups something glorious will occur

JUDGMENT.

JUDGMENT
Card number 20

Traditional Points About the Card

This card shows all the cycles of life: birth, death, Karma, and reincarnation. Its divinatory meaning is life's lessons must be learned in order to evolve spiritually.

Modern Meaning

When this card appears in a spread, the querent is learning lessons that the spirit world wishes her to understand. It always promises a light at the end of the tunnel, so if things are really upside-down in her life, this card gives her hope and tries to make her realize that she is simply in a classroom situation.

Reversed

The querent is a confused soul who has lost her way in life. A cantankerous elderly person will cause trouble.

Key Points

- the karma card
- take what life brings
- reincarnation
- spiritual lessons to learn

THE WORLD
Card number 21

THE WORLD.

Traditional Points About the Card

The World frequently illustrates a woman dancing, dressed in lilac or purple. The laurel leaf represents victory, the bull indicates strength, the lion suggests intelligence, the eagle symbolizes the seeing eye, and the man signifies an angel and spiritual power.

Modern Meaning

This card symbolizes perfection and completion. It's a highly successful card, as it brings victory and all good things with it. This also suggests travel around the world. I sometimes use this card to tell the querent that the world is her oyster and that she should not be afraid of taking a chance. Victory and success are noticeable in her future.

Reversed

The querent is in a rut and cannot see what lessons she must learn. Advise her to change her life.

Key Points

- success and victory
- travel usually abroad
- perfection
- the world is your oyster

3

THE SUIT OF CUPS

The suit of Cups is the first suit of the minor arcana. These cards give the details that bring a reading to life. They fill in the gaps and allow you to stretch your imagination, making each reading individual. There are fifty-six cards discussed in the next four chapters, and they make up the four suits: Cups, Wands, Swords, and Pentacles.

The suit of Cups is the nicest of all the four suits. It focuses mainly on relationships and family matters, giving meanings to all types of situations. A number of Cups gives a positive slant to a spread of cards and it often brings lighter aspects to a sad or harsh reading.

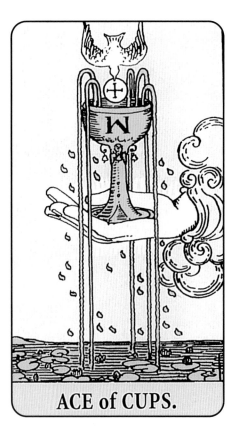

ACE of CUPS.

ACE OF CUPS
Card number 23

Traditional Points About the Card

The hand of God is clasping the cup, demonstrating that it is a gift from the heavens. The dove is a symbol of stillness and serenity.

Modern Meaning

This is the second-best card in the deck. Very soon, the querent will experience joy and peace. You will need to look at the surrounding cards to ascertain the reason for her good fortune. If bad cards are at hand, then this card will bring about a happy outcome to a current problem. The querent will hear of a pregnancy or she will celebrate someone's engagement or wedding. All will be well, because this is a truly wonderful card.

Reversed

Things have not always been the way they should be, but with hard work, good fortune will come along.

Key Points

- the second-best card in the deck
- births, weddings, engagements, and celebrations
- a happy outcome

TWO OF CUPS
Card number 14

Traditional Points About the Card

A man and woman are present on the card, and some traditions suggest that the woman is pregnant.

Modern Meaning

Some say that this is the card of soul mates or two extremely compatible individuals. If the querent is single, then a wonderful new romance is on the way. She will be comfortable in her relationship and compatible with her partner. The union will be sexy but also based on truth and honesty. The couple communicates very well, making it not just a physical connection but also a blending of the minds. This card points toward an impending marriage or engagement and a pregnancy.

If you are reading for a person who has split up from her partner, there should soon be reconciliation.

Reversed

A breakdown in relationships is suggested.

Key Points

- wonderful relationship of mind and body
- reconciliation
- engagement, marriage, or pregnancy

THREE OF CUPS
Card number 25

Traditional Points About the Card

Three young women are celebrating by eating, drinking, and having a good time.

Modern Meaning

This is a joyous card. Parties and celebrations will be evident in the coming year for the individual, with births, weddings, or other occasions coming along. It is also the card of a family reunion. Any problems in the querent's life will soon conclude, so tell her not to worry. If your querent is romantically unattached, a new love affair will lift her spirits. If the querent is married or in a relationship, everything will be rosy.

Reversed

The querent is in a relationship with love for the wrong reasons, too much sex, and not enough communication.

If the querent overindulges with food and drink, her weight will rocket. Difficult people are around the querent, and there is backbiting within the family.

Key Points

- celebrations in the family or with friends
- problems solved
- new love affairs or harmony in marriage

FOUR OF CUPS
Card number 26

Traditional Points About the Card

This image shows a person sitting alone with a "couldn't care less" attitude.

Modern Meaning

The querent or someone close to her is dissatisfied and thinking that the grass must be greener on the other side. A family upset is expected, maybe in a relationship, or there may be problems generally in the family. Help and encouragement will be offered from an unexpected source, giving her a much happier outcome than she expects.

Reversed

The querent will feel like giving up and she could let a great opportunity pass by her. Tell her to try to make new friends and get out more

Key Points

- family upsets or problems with relationships
- the querent must try to be grateful for what she has
- help and support are at hand

FIVE OF CUPS
Card number 27

Traditional Points About the Card

Depending on the deck, the person on this card usually looks run-down, with feelings of regret and unhappiness. There are cups at his feet with spilled liquid pouring from them, but he does not see the two cups standing up behind him. The birds flying overhead signify the human soul.

Modern Meaning

Most Cups cards are happy ones, but this one is quite depressive, especially if it is with relationship cards. A separation is likely for the querent, and children could be involved. She will regret her past actions and want to turn the clock back. This also means unrequited love.

If it sits next to work or financial cards, a business will crumble or money problems will cause despair. Sometimes, and only in rare cases, the client or someone associated with her could feel suicidal. If you think this is the case, you have to take it seriously. There is a lot to offer in life, and support and guidance is there for her. She must hold her head up high and look around, because things are not as bad as they seem. You must always give your client hope, and stress that eventually there will be a positive outcome.

Reversed

The querent will be meeting people from the past. There may be a house move.

Key Points

- looking into the past
- regret, intense sadness
- problems with business or money
- unrequited love

SIX OF CUPS
Card number 28

Traditional Points About the Card

Most decks depict a couple on this card. The woman appears to be declining the man's offers.

Modern Meaning

A reunion is likely. Some decks refer to this as being a love affair from the past that will be rekindled, or reconciliation in a relationship. There are definitely conflicts and arguments, and the man may be trying to win over the woman. If you have established that the querent is divorced, it is possible that there will be an upset around the custody of a child or arguments over money.

Where the querent has children of teenage years, then an innocent love affair will start. In most cases, this will begin as two young people starting out as friends and becoming romantically involved later. Their relationship will be of a nonsexual kind unless the Lovers appears in the same spread.

Reversed

A small inheritance or windfall is possible. The querent or someone near her is a person who refuses to grow up.

Key Points

- relationships from the past
- reconciliation
- conflict and quarrels around relationships
- marriage disputes over custody
- in young people, an innocent affair

SEVEN OF CUPS
Card number 29

Traditional Points About the Card

One of the seven cups contains a snake or asp: this represents the lowest spiritual force. The wreath with a ribbon attached to it is a sign of victory and success. A jeweled butterfly is representative of the soul. On the highest level is a dragon, which epitomizes anger and conflict. The final cup holds a castle, which suggests that the querent's soul is growing karmically.

Modern Meaning

This is a very spiritual and psychic card. Tell the querent to interpret or write down her dreams, because she will find it easy to connect with her spirit guides and she will find herself experiencing some psychic visions.

There will be many choices for her to make in the coming year, so prepare her for changes, which in turn will take her on to a new learning curve. Positive things are ahead, so looking forward to these experiences will open a new chapter in her life.

Reversed

The reversed meaning is the same as the upright meaning.

Key Points

• choices and decisions
• listen to dream sleep, await new beginnings

EIGHT OF CUPS
Card number 30

Traditional Points About the Card

Eight cups stand on the ground while a cloaked figure runs away, so this points to someone who is running away from her past. All eights in tarot predict good luck.

Modern Meaning

When this card appears in a spread, your client may be looking back into the past too much and not living for today. It is also the card of moving on and taking a different direction. If the Lovers or the Two of Cups are close by, the client may have to think about whether she wants to remain . . . or leave a relationship.

A blonde woman will come into the life of the querent. Look at the additional cards in the spread to decide whether she is good or bad.

Reversed

The querent is feeling sorry for oneself. She may encounter
a very selfish and egotistical person.

Key Points

• moving away from situations
• new beginnings
• not living in the past
• all eights in tarot bring good luck and hope

NINE OF CUPS
Card number 31

Traditional Points About the Card

The plump man on this card shows a person reveling in the good life. Well-fed and happy, he enjoys all the things life has to offer. The nine upright cups behind him signify abundance. The Romany Gypsies call this "the Wish Card"

Modern Meaning

Being the wish card, this is truly positive. Whenever this card comes out in a spread, it illustrates that the client's wishes will be granted. Give her hope in foretelling that her future will be joyful and that a celebration is at the forefront. Tell the querent to wish for what she wants, as in time she will get it. Some readers like to ask the querent to make a silent wish upon the card.

Reversed

The querent may be susceptible to overeating, drinking, and weight gain. Others take advantage of the querent's hospitality or good nature.

Key Points

- the Wish Card
- make a wish
- celebrations
- abundance

TEN OF CUPS
Card number 32

Traditional Points About the Card

You can see a family illustrated on this card. Sometimes a rainbow is present, meaning joy and purpose.

Modern Meaning

This card denotes a good relationship or love partnership. The couple may have had difficulties, but now they find happiness and stability. They will still have to work at their marriage, though, because life often brings about difficulties. If the lovers make an effort, they will be happy, successful, and even more closely united than they are now. If you are reading for a single woman, then you can predict this relationship for her future.

The card can also predict a windfall when next to the Nine of Pentacles. This may be only a very small amount of money or goods, but it could also be huge. Only predict a large win if you are certain about it.

Reversed

A family upset will result in a child running away. Romantic tiffs and squabbles will go on for at least six months. If next to the Nine or Ten of Swords, there will be news of a death.

Key Points

- relationship and marriage card
- a windfall or a large win
- bad relationships in the past, but true happiness comes later after lovers work hard to make each other happy

PAGE OF CUPS
Card number 33

PAGE of CUPS.

Traditional Points About the Card

This card represents a child who might have blue or hazel eyes and fair or mousy hair. Naturally, the coloring would depend upon the race. In some decks, this page represents a girl, but traditionally pages can be either sex.

Modern Meaning

The child is connected to the querent in some way, so this might symbolize a child that she has now or one that she will have in the future. If this is not possible due to the age or condition of the querent, then it would represent a relative such as a niece, nephew, or grandchild.

Personality

This page is sweet-natured and will not usually bring any problems to the family. She will love her home life and be sociable with friends and relations. She will not be particularly academic and could struggle a bit at school, but later in life she will get by and go on to hold a practical position in employment.

The Page of Cups usually enjoys projects such as the arts or a gentle form of sport. This might include dancing, singing, music, the arts, stage, theater, martial arts, or pool.

This is a very psychic young person, so tell the querent to expect her to have imaginary friends or talk about God and angels from an early age. The card talks about an endearing little person that any family would be proud to include in it.

As a Situation

This card can represent a course, lessons, and learning something new that might be artistic or creative.

Reversed

This card in the reversed position signifies a change in a child's character

Key Points

- can represent a female child in some decks
- has a tendency to be psychic
- a child who enjoys mild sport and the arts

KNIGHT OF CUPS
Card number 34

KNIGHT of CUPS.

Traditional Points About the Card

This card represents a young man between the ages of seventeen and twenty-nine. In white races, his eyes are usually blue to hazel and his hair color can be either sandy blond or mousey.

Modern Meaning

This young man is a favorite with women due to his charm and good looks. He oozes charisma and can usually have any girl he chooses. He is rarely faithful to his partner and will have left a trail of heartbroken females in his past. Being highly sexed, racy, and smart, he's the "love 'em and leave 'em" type, who is not opposed to overindulging with drink and drugs.

This young man might have a history of trouble with the law. He may also have a poor school record because he could not (or would not) concentrate on academic matters. He is a loveable rogue who in time will eventually follow the right path. His generosity ensures that he has many friends, but he will not be as faithful to them as they are to him.

In many cases, if the querent is a mature woman, this is a son. Always give hope for the future for this knight, as he rarely turns out to be a bad person in the end.

As a Situation

This card can represent visitors, company, visiting friends, day trips, and outings.

Reversed

The Knight of Cups will lose his lover to another man. If two or more male character cards are present in a spread with the Knight of Cups, he has to fight for something or he feels threatened in some way.

Key Points

- a womanizer
- an unfaithful lover
- dabbling in petty crime
- drugs and fast cars
- a change of character in later life

QUEEN OF CUPS
Card number 35

QUEEN of CUPS.

Traditional Points About the Card

This queen is usually blue- to hazel-eyed with light brown hair, depending upon racial considerations. Her age can range from seventeen up.

Modern Meaning

This is a mature woman with a loving, gentle personality. She is a maternal figure, enjoying home life and children. She can sometimes be too soft, so she allows others to take her good nature for granted. In certain cases, she has been divorced and will find her true love only later in life, when she has become stronger in her opinions. She shows fondness for animals and a love of nature. She has great perception, with brilliant intuition, and her common sense will always lead her away from trouble. She will not welcome outsiders immediately, but once you have won her confidence she is a friend for life.

As a Situation

The social life picks up and good times with friends are on the way.

Reversed

This can relate to a horrible mother-in-law or stepmother or a gossipy and interfering woman who exaggerates all the time.

Key Points

- lovely-natured maternal figure
- love of animals
- likes her home, creature comforts, and children
- may be divorced

KING of CUPS.

KING OF CUPS
Card number 36

Traditional Points About the Card

This man has blue to hazel eyes (depending upon his race), and he has an air of authority about him.

Modern Meaning

This king is ambitious, and he is accountable in business. He shows a strong and powerful image, giving accurate advice while counseling others. This king may occasionally put others down. Sometimes he is inconsiderate in marriage, being quiet and noncommunicative, far different from the man we see at work.

A private person who keeps his thoughts very much to himself, he gives little of his inner self away, even to his nearest and dearest. He will have to try harder with marriage and commitment, as his wife may find him dull and boring. However, he is a reliable father who is solid and steady, and in some cases, religious.

As a Situation

New male friends are likely, but these acquaintances will be short-lived.

Reversed

This man may be a marriage cheat. He can be controlling and manipulative. He is a man's man who likes to drink with his friends.

Key Points

- ambitious, responsible, and a good counselor at home
- noncommunicative, dull, and boring
- a father figure

4

THE SUIT OF WANDS

Recognized in most decks as wands, batons, or rods, this suit is associated with work, career, and business matters. If more than three wands appear in the same spread, the querent has her career, business, job, or even a voluntary occupation in the forefront of her mind at the time of the reading.

ACE of WANDS.

ACE OF WANDS
Card number 37

Traditional Points About the Card

A single rod sits in the center of the card. In some decks, branches grow from the rod to symbolize growth and rebirth. The hand of God is bearing gifts.

Modern Meaning

All aces in tarot are optimistic, and this card is always pleasant to see in a spread. This gives the querent a new beginning or discovery to look forward to, as it always signifies something good. In most cases, this can be a new job or a new start in property or business. If the ace is among other Rod cards, it could relate to a situation around work (look to surrounding cards to establish whether they are good or bad). This card can also predict fertility or a possible birth.

Reversed

This card can indicate a block or delay.

Key Points

- a brand new job or business venture
- fertility and birth

TWO OF WANDS
Card number 38

Traditional Points About the Card

A young man holds in his hand a rod bearing leaves and acorns. A crystal ball is in his other hand to give him the wisdom to make the correct choices in life.

Modern Meaning

As twos in tarot represent choices and decisions, this card can indicate the need to make a serious decision at work or business. A new venture is ahead, but it is up to the querent to take up the challenge or leave it alone, as it does not appear to be a matter of destiny.

Sometimes this can mean making a great effort at work, especially if disruptive cards are present in the spread. The querent may contemplate buying something new, such as a new vehicle or an expensive gift for someone else.

Reversed

Have patience because delays and setbacks are imminent. The querent will lose interest in work or business, and mundane tasks will become boring.

Key Points

- choices in work and business
- struggles and problems
- purchasing new things or buying gifts

THREE OF WANDS
Card number 39

Traditional Points About the Card

A figure stands with three wands surrounding him. He supports the wands, indicating that he lifts the spirits of those around him.

Modern Meaning

The querent may help or support a friend or relative. The energy that she expends by propping up those around her will make her feel worn out and tired. Carrying people through difficult times is fine up to a point, but not if it is sapping the querent's own energy. If you are reading for someone who cannot stand up for herself, she will seek help and support from others, but she will rarely act on the advice that they give her.

Another meaning to this card is that work and business will improve. In some cases, work brings travel.

Reversed

The querent is wasting her talents and listening to bad advice.

Key Points

- advice and support given or received
- improvements in career, work, and business

FOUR OF WANDS
Card number 40

Traditional Points About the Card

Four wands stand tall, symbolizing the four walls of a home or the security within it. There is usually some indication of family life with this card.

Modern Meaning

In some tarot decks, this card is associated with marriage or a relationship where the people are living together. As wands represent work, this relationship may need hard work for it to succeed. There may have been difficulties in the past or they may occur in the future. The couple can repair past damage if they are prepared to make an effort. Encourage the querent to fulfill her ambitions and to count her blessings.

Reversed

Relationships will fail. The querent is spending too much money.

Key Points

- marriage or committed relationship
- hard work improves a relationship
- fulfill ambitions

FIVE OF WANDS
Card number 41

Traditional Points About the Card

Five wands bearing people are competing against each other. Each figure's mode of dress is different, suggesting a diversity of opinions.

Modern Meaning

There are problems and battles at work. Colleagues around the querent are outraged about work matters, and there is no peace, quiet, or harmony. This represents a trying time. Encourage the client to be strong and not to submit to bullying or backstabbing. Life may be unpleasant for a while.

Reversed

The querent is at her very lowest, but things will improve. She must leave things as they are or walk away from them. She can try and sort things out in her present situation or find a new one later.

Key Points

- battles at work
- bullying and backstabbing
- colleagues up in arms

SIX OF WANDS
Card number 42

Traditional Points About the Card

A proud man rides on horseback with six wands surrounding him. He holds a rod laced with a red ribbon, indicating virtue. The wreath of victory is by his side.

Modern Meaning

The querent may have had tough times in the past and may still be struggling. The surrounding cards will show what the problems are, but whatever they might be, this card predicts victory to follow. Ensure the client that her difficulties will be short-lived.

This card can also mean good news coming—or buying or exchanging an automobile. If the card is among many Sword cards, it can mean problems with a vehicle.

Reversed

Victory is delayed or lost. The querent may want something that belongs to someone else.

Key Points

- struggles at first, victory to follow
- good news to come
- changing vehicles or automobile problems

SEVEN OF WANDS
Card number 43

Traditional Points About the Card

A man stands with six wands around or before him and one in his hand. He observes this thoughtfully.

Modern Meaning

This card can refer to two opposing ideas, one being redundancy and the other being a promotion. If negative cards surround the seven of wands, the meaning is loss and being fired, but if positive cards are present, the seven of wands predicts a promotion. If the querent cannot foresee a promotion happening in her current occupation, this indicates a change of job that takes her higher up the ladder or one that pays better. Encourage her not to walk away from her difficulties but to face them, because only then will all be well.

The seven of wands can also indicate that the client will soon be teaching or training others—that is, transferring information to others.

Reversed

The querent may experience an embarrassing incident. Someone may try to show the querent up or make her feel small in front of others.

Key Points

- promotion or loss of job
- teaching or training
- learning to face difficulties

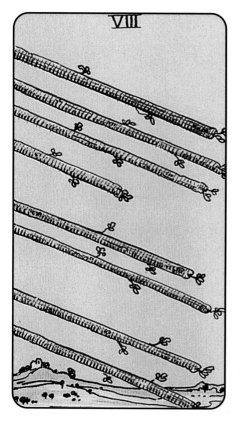

EIGHT OF WANDS
Card number 44

Traditional Points About the Card

Eight wands fly through lush vegetation and landscape. The river alludes to nature and time.

Modern Meaning

This is one of the travel cards, but mainly it refers to air travel. Even though wands usually represent work, this journey is likely to be for pleasure, so the querent may soon be able to take a well-deserved vacation. A house move also works with this card, so you could predict that the querent will not always stay where she is now.

When you apply this card to a work situation, it means advancement unless the card is reversed. Changes are coming, but they will move slowly at the start and speed up later.

Reversed

There may be a strike action at work. The querent cancels a vacation. There may be some jealousy at work and some arguments at work or at home.

Key Points

- journey by plane
- changes coming swiftly after a long wait
- a house move
- advancement or problems at work

NINE OF WANDS
Card number 45

Traditional Points About the Card

A figure stands with eight wands behind him and one to the side of him. You can interpret this as saying that the wands are protecting him in case he needs to defend himself.

Modern Meaning

This is the card of caution, so the querent must be on her guard. A time waster or sneaky person will be among the querent's or her partner's friends. Look at the other cards in the spread to determine the situation and the outcome. Small groups of people could gang together to bring the querent down.

Reversed

A person in the family might have a drinking or drug problem.

Key Points

The querent must be on her guard. Time wasters are around. Groups may gang up against the querent.

TEN OF WANDS
Card number 46

Traditional Points About the Card

A man struggles to carry the wands on his shoulders. The feather in his hat represents his determination to see a project through to completion no matter what.

Modern Meaning

The querent needs to keep her nose to the grindstone for a while because she will need to work hard in order to finish a task or to please her superiors. At work, someone may ask her to take on extra responsibility, and she could find others taking her for granted. If this Rod card appears around relationship cards, her partner steps up the pressure and leaves her feeling emotionally and physically exhausted. This card can sometimes mean that the querent is in a dead-end job.

Reversed

The querent is waiting for a promotion. The querent may have a legacy stolen. She may experience broken bones or injuries.

Key Points

- hard work and toil
- taking a lot of responsibility
- pressure; not getting anywhere at work

PAGE OF WANDS
Card number 47

PAGE of WANDS.

Traditional Points About the Card

A youth in plain clothing holds a single rod tightly in his hands. The feathers in his hat symbolize the gods in the Egyptian pantheon.

Modern Meaning

In most decks, this page can be either male or female, but very often the Page of Wands is a young boy from the age of birth to fifteen. He is a lovely, inquisitive child with a lively nature, and he is easy to manage. This could be the querent's son or a relative. Listen to what a child has to say, because he could be the bearer of good news.

As a Situation

This card could represent news, correspondence, or writing something important.

Reversed

Illness, bad news, and rumors fall heavily on the querent's shoulders. Childish pranks and impatient friends may annoy the querent.

Key Points

- girl or boy, but the male sex is usually accurate
- fair-haired or light-eyed in appropriate races
- enjoyable child related to querent
- good news is ahead

THE KNIGHT OF WANDS
Card number 48

KNIGHT of WANDS.

Traditional Points About the Card

A knight dressed in armor carries a rod placed over his right shoulder. In some decks, there is a dragon on his helmet, indicating aggression and battles.

Modern Meaning

In white races, this knight usually has blue or green eyes and his hair is blond to medium brown. He has the gift of gab and he is a "Jack the Lad" character, but he is also rather traditional. The Knights of Wands and Cups can sometimes be erratic, but they tend to settle down in later life. During his late teens and early twenties, he will change jobs frequently, hop in and out of bed with a variety of partners, and carry on regardless, without a care in the world. Sometimes his rather senseless attitude lands him in hot water.

His excellent conversational skills ensure that his opinions are sometimes fixed or inflexible, so others see his lack of tact as offensive. The truth of the matter is that he is a nice young man who will blossom when he reaches full maturity.

As a Situation

This card signifies travel and communication, especially for business purposes.

Reversed

There is an insecure young man who breaks promises somewhere around the querent. He is someone who cannot resist temptation.

Key Points

- blond to brown hair where appropriate
- light eyes where appropriate
- restless, with frequent job changes
- traditional views
- chatty; gift of gab
- could occasionally put his foot in his mouth

QUEEN OF WANDS
Card number 49

Traditional Points About the Card

A light-eyed woman stands in the open countryside. Usually her gold-colored hair is highlighted on this card, indicating the color of the sun.

Modern Meaning

The Queen of Wands is generally nice, and, loving nature and animals, she will probably have a houseful of pets. She loves her home and makes a near-perfect wife and mother. Green issues interest her, and she is always prepared to do her share for any good causes that arise. If her partner does not give her the attention she needs, she could be prone to flirt or even to embark on an affair, but her partner will have to push her to the extreme for her to go this far.

As a Situation

The querent will take advice and then make sensible business or financial decisions.

Reversed

The querent may be or may have around her a fast and loose woman who is temperamental and fickle. She has no interest in family life.

101

Key Points

- sincere, lovely woman
- blue-eyed where appropriate
- red/blond hair where appropriate
- loves animals and nature
- good wife and mother
- could be prone to an affair in extreme cases

KING of WANDS.

KING OF WANDS
Card number 50

Traditional Points About the Card

A man is standing tall and looking out over the countryside. His rich crown shows us that he is spiritually developed.

Modern Meaning

This king is pleasant and generally liked by all. He is an honest, reliable, amusing man with a witty personality. He is sweet-natured and especially geared toward his family and friends. He is usually faithful, but, like the queen, will always need to be kept interested romantically. This king is intelligent and does well at work or in business. He is an excellent boss or employer and is fair and sympathetic. At best he shares the decision-making with his partner, but he can be weak-willed at times and happy to leave her to make all the decisions. He is a great father, and his wife can rely on him, though he can be a bit soft and allow their children to run riot. A daughter could wrap him around her little finger.

As a Situation

There will be communications and negotiations that lead to success.

Reversed

This man could be a liar with a devious and unreliable attitude. Lots of broken promises and arguments could occur within the family.

Key Points

- fair to brown hair in appropriate races
- blue or gray eyes in appropriate races
- intelligent, reliable, amusing, and witty
- good father and husband, but a little soft at times
- usually faithful

5

THE SUIT OF SWORDS

Unfortunately, this suit is rather depressing, because swords represent conflict, illness, and tension. If someone is going through a particularly bad time, many swords can be present in a spread. It is always best to follow a "difficult" reading with something positive; otherwise, the querent will go away with little hope.

ACE of SWORDS.

ACE OF SWORDS
Card number 51

Traditional Points About the Card

The hand of God holds a double-edged sword. This represents justice on higher levels. The crown, from which the laurel palm and red and white roses emerge, is a sign of great spiritual action.

Modern Meaning

This card tells us that the querent has recently endured trouble or hardship and may be down in the dumps or—in extreme cases—depressed. She has learned some valuable lessons through these difficult times and now victory will follow. Give your client hope if you feel that she is dejected, and tell her that she will soon discover that her life is back on track. This card links with hospitals and operations, especially when the Five of Pentacles is in the spread. If the Tower appears too, this Ace may signify a wound that needs stitches.

Reversed

Fate and destiny will take their course. The querent must beware of making wrong decisions. Delays and shocks may come to the querent.

Key Points

- struggle at first but victory follows
- if next to the Five of Pentacles, an operation
- if next to the Tower, stitches to a wound

TWO OF SWORDS
Card number 52

Traditional Points About the Card

A woman stands blindfolded while holding two crossed swords. She cannot see things around her clearly. Tradition calls this "the divorce card"!

Modern Meaning

At some point in the future, the querent will experience severe relationship problems. A once-happy marriage or partnership starts to turn sour, and a hopeless outcome for the relationship is inevitable. An infidelity or future infidelity will take place if the Lovers, the Three of Swords, or the Devil is in the spread. The querent must sit down and make a conscious decision as to whether she will continue with the relationship. Whatever she decides, the outcome will definitely end in a break in the relationship.

It is worth noting that this scenario can also apply to a business partnership or even to a project that the querent should off-load.

T i p

If you hope to be a professional reader, be very careful when making predictions with this card. You could be reading for someone that has just embarked on a new romance or recently entered into marriage. In many cases, this card carries a long-term prediction. The querent may still be in the throes of true love, so telling her that the relationship will eventually end could upset her unnecessarily. A good way to use this card is to say that her relationship will include some difficulties and that later on, she will have to make decisions as to how it is to continue. Even though you may know that the end is near, it must always be the querent's decision to break up. Never predict that her partner will leave her.

R e v e r s e d

Do not be pushed into making a decision.

K e y   P o i n t s

- divorce or separations in relationships
- choices and decisions
- blocked situations

THREE OF SWORDS
Card number 53

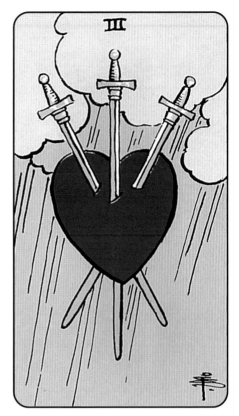

Traditional Points About the Card

The illustration shows a heart pierced by three swords. This symbolizes three people in a relationship. Tradition tells us that this is "the adultery card."

Modern Meaning

This is only the adultery card when the Lovers card appears in the same spread. The querent does not have to be married; she may just live with someone. If you are going to predict adultery, always state that it is the querent's decision to remain true or to be false. Although the spirits may bring someone new into her life, this is a test for her and it is her choice at the end of the day. She does not have to embark on an affair; she has the option to walk away from it. This sad card indicates that the querent is not happy and that her life could continue to be miserable for a while.

If the Three of Swords is next to the Empress, there may be news of a miscarriage. If it appears with cards that talk about health matters, someone around the querent may have heart problems or angina.

Oddly enough, an alternative meaning can sometimes indicate a house move.

Reversed

The querent may experience loneliness and confusion.

Key Points

- adultery, if with the Lovers card
- with cards of health—heart problems
- with the Empress card—miscarriage
- upset and misery
- a house move

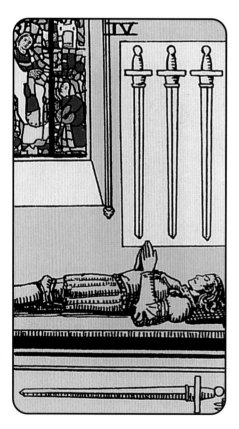

FOUR OF SWORDS
Card number 54

Traditional Points About the Card

A knight is lying on a coffin by a window. He is separating himself from the world outside.

Modern Meaning

This is one of the many health cards, as it supposes that the querent or someone close to her is convalescing. It does not necessarily talk of a serious illness, as this is more likely to be a virus or minor problem. However, she will still retreat from the outside world, probably by taking time off from work. This is also a waiting time, so it is essential that the querent be patient. Fate will control everything in the end, so assure the querent that the future is in the hands of the spirit world.

Reversed

Put life on pause for a while and learn to be patient.

Key Points

- convalescing at home
- taking sick time off due to minor illness
- fate and destiny rules and controls, so learn to be patient

FIVE OF SWORDS
Card number 55

Traditional Points About the Card

A hooded figure looks at a scene of hopelessness. He holds three swords, meaning that he is in control of the outcome and that he must change things for the better. Not all is lost.

Modern Meaning

This card relates to health and especially a time of mental strain and pressure that leaves the querent living on her nerves for a while. This card also has an angry air about it, depicting violence and hostility. Often the root of this problem is a relationship, so the querent may suffer mental or physical abuse from a partner. People may spread gossip about the querent or there may be family quarrels. In rare situations, there might be a burglary or break-in for the querent or for someone she knows.

A positive aspect of this card says that an admirer will show up within a twelve-month period.

Reversed

The querent may be experiencing a feeling of doom and gloom. She may be ignoring good advice.

Key Points

- mental or nervous health problems
- family quarrels, gossiping
- violence or abusive arguments around relationships
- burglaries
- an admirer

SIX OF SWORDS
Card number 56

Traditional Points About the Card

A man directs a boat along choppy water toward calmer waters, which suggests that things will be brighter ahead.

Modern Meaning

This card is associated with movement, which could imply moving house, changing a job, changing a relationship, or just moving on to better things. You can predict that the querent will move out of her current area—perhaps only a few miles away or to a distant place. The Six of Swords can represent an overseas vacation, especially if other travel cards are around. This card signifies the end of problems and soothing times ahead.

Reversed

There may be delays around a house move or around travel. A vacation may be postponed.

Key Points

• a house move out of the area
• a holiday and better times ahead

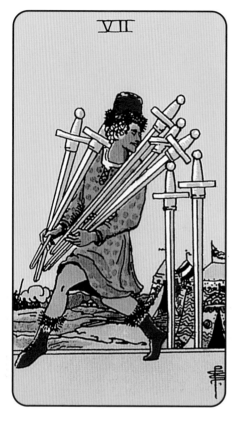

SEVEN OF SWORDS
Card number 57

Traditional Points About the Card

A man with a covered face, who is not clearly visible, indicates that someone is not showing his true colors. Tradition considers this a card of criminality or of cloak-and-dagger events.

Modern Meaning

This is not a nice card, as it can mean theft, which can be anything from a burglary to a snatched purse, a swindle, or some other kind of loss. If this card is around pages, it points toward a child who is stealing. Once again, be cautious when predicting a burglary. Some people may panic at the thought of this, but the querent may simply hear of a break-in rather than have one herself.

This card also denotes jealousy. Someone around the querent may be envious or vindictive, but he will be clever enough to hide his true colors. Warn the client about false friends or manipulative colleagues.

Reversed

Things that were lost may turn up. The querent will make up with a loved one.

Key Points

- theft and deception
- trickery and jealousy

EIGHT OF SWORDS
Card number 58

Traditional Points About the Card

A woman stands bound, with eight swords surrounding her, and she cannot move. A blind-fold tells us that she cannot or will not see the truth.

Modern Meaning

The querent will be in a very confused state of mind, knowing inwardly that something is wrong but not wanting to confront the situation. This usually indicates relationship difficulties or work problems. Karmically speaking, these tough lessons will make the querent face up to her weaknesses and become stronger as a result. There may also be a female around the querent who wants to hurt her or to exact revenge.

Reversed

The querent should keep her chin up and all will soon be well. Negative feelings fade.

Key Points

- feelings of being trapped
- confusion
- a female is out for revenge
- karma, learning spiritual lessons

NINE OF SWORDS
Card number 59

Traditional Points About the Card

The figure's hands are tied, symbolic of the things that we cannot control.

Modern Meaning

This card can mean death, but the same rules apply here as for the Death card in the major arcana. Actual death is only relevant when the card falls next to the Tower, which means a sudden death—perhaps from a heart attack or a car crash. This situation is very rare, so you are unlikely to see this combination often. Because the reading is so extreme, you must play it down where possible. When the Nine of Swords appears without the Tower in the same reading, the querent will feel trapped or circumstances around her will appear to be hopeless. She could also experience problems in connection with a mother or mother-in-law.

Reversed

There is always a rainbow after the storm. Good news coming at last.

Key Points

- death if the Tower is also present
- hopeless situations
- problems with mother or mother-in-law figure

TEN OF SWORDS
Card number 60

Traditional Points About the Card

A man lies helpless and bleeding with ten swords piercing him. Snow falls from a black sky, portraying a hopeless day. Tradition calls either the Nine or the Ten of Swords "death cards."

Modern Meaning

I regard this card as the worst one in the deck because it gives very little hope. If this appears in a reading, you should concentrate on the surrounding cards. If the Ten of Swords and the Death card appear anywhere in the same spread, then the death of someone or something is highly probable. On its own, it can mean financial loss resulting from either bad luck, job loss, or in exceptional situations, even bankruptcy. Ill health could be a factor. Try your best to give hope to the querent and always follow through with something positive.

Reversed

A karmic debt has been paid. The querent should feel hopeful and encouraged because she will have spiritual protection throughout bad times.

Key Points

- Ten of Swords with the Death card implies a death
- ill health, hospital and sickness
- financial loss
- misery

THE PAGE OF SWORDS
Card number 61

Traditional Points About the Card

A child stands strong, holding a sword upright, ready for battle.

PAGE of SWORDS.

Modern Meaning

This page can be male or female and he can be quite difficult to control. He tends to be willful and full of his own opinions. He can also be stubborn, and he may find discipline hard to accept. His parents will constantly battle to gain control of him, and at times they will be at the end of their tether. In some cases, the child may have a hyperactive disorder such as ADHD, so it might be necessary to encourage the querent to have him examined by a specialist. This child might have a spiteful nature, which will get him into hot water with teachers and those who have to take care of him. In teenage years, he might get into trouble with the law!

It really does depend on how you wish to interpret this child's card when doing a reading. You may feel that he is just somewhat excitable—for example, a very young child who is going through the "terrible twos." However, he will always be a handful, and the querent will need to guide him along the correct path in life. His good qualities are that he gives a lot of love and that he will grow up to be a very capable person.

As a Situation

Important news is coming, or the querent will sign a contract or other important document.

Reversed

Try to understand a sick or mentally ill child who might be physically or mentally handicapped.

Key Points

- Child's nature—difficult, hyperactive, naughty, and opinionated
- Can be either male or female

THE KNIGHT OF SWORDS
Card number 62

KNIGHT of SWORDS.

Traditional Points About the Card

A dark, dangerous-looking knight stands tall with a sword, signifying his strength of mind.

Modern Meaning

This knight is a fearless, confident person who has little or no conscience. When he sets his mind to what he wants, he will stop at nothing to achieve his goals, not caring whose toes he treads on along the way. He is usually nice-looking but deep and mysterious, as he does not allow anyone to get close to him. Women want him because he is sexual and extremely passionate. As is the case with most of the knights, this young man tends to be rather full of himself.

As a Situation

Travel is likely, possibly without much prior warning, as are last-minute arrangements and quick decisions.

Reversed

The querent should wait and be patient.

Key Points

- dark in coloring
- mysterious, deep
- sexual, passionate, and ambitious
- journeys and travel

QUEEN of SWORDS.

QUEEN OF SWORDS
Card number 63

Traditional Points About the Card

A dark-haired woman sits and stares ahead with an upraised sword in her hand. The red roses are symbolic of her passion, but her sharp, spiked crown suggests that she has an edge to her.

Modern Meaning

Although this woman can have a sharp tongue at times, she is the type that seems to have everything under control. She is a strong, self-sufficient woman who is in tune with most things around her. She is career-oriented and enjoys her work. She is nobody's fool and tends not to trust men much. Men admire her because she has physical beauty as well as spiritual beauty. She may have had previous difficulties in her life and has become cynical.

She does have a gentle side and tends to be a well-balanced mother, giving her children the independence they need and the chance of finding their own way in life.

As a Situation

There may be conflict and the querent may have to stand up for herself against difficult people.

Reversed

The querent or someone around her may be intolerant, interfering, and oblivious to others' opinions.

Key Points

- strong, career-oriented
- has had a hard life
- doesn't trust men
- a well-balanced mother
- divorced or widowed

KING of SWORDS.

KING OF SWORDS
Card number 64

Traditional Points About the Card

A serious-looking king stands firmly holding a double-edged sword. This represents true justice.

Modern Meaning

This man is usually a popular, well-liked individual who is intellectual and generally at the top of his profession. Because of his capabilities in dealing with company politics and his extreme determination in all he does, the King of Swords will always thrive in business. This card can also correspond to professionals, such as doctors, teachers, or members of the armed forces. He is not particularly spiritual but shows no skepticism either.

As a Situation

The querent will consult a lawyer, doctor, builder, or someone who has special knowledge or skills.

Reversed

This card can represent a bully who misuses his power, a stern husband or father, or a disloyal and secretive man.

Key Points

- an admired man
- dark eyes, dark hair
- political rather than spiritual

6

THE SUIT OF PENTACLES

In many decks, the designer calls this suit Coins or Discs. This suit is associated with money, study, and work. The Pentacles rarely predict severe or long-term problems. If you see more than three Pentacle cards in a spread, the querent might have a thirst for money or she might simply be in business or dealing with financial and business matters.

ACE of PENTACLES.

ACE OF PENTACLES
Card number 65

Traditional Points About the Card

A hand is holding a shining pentacle surrounded by growth and flowers. This symbolizes God bestowing well-deserved wealth in return for past efforts.

Modern Meaning

This is the best money card in tarot. Even if unpleasant financial cards are in a spread, this promises that the querent's guide will take care of her financially. Give the querent hope and inform her that money will soon be flowing freely. New projects and new moneymaking ideas will succeed. Aces are always positive, so look forward to a fresh start or even a new address.

If this card appears with the Wheel of Fortune, then the querent will receive a legacy or some money through an insurance claim. Next to the Nine of Pentacles, this card indicates that a large lump sum of cash will turn up. In rare cases, this can denote a lottery win, but this combination can equally apply when a person sells a house.

Reversed

The querent will suffer from greed, materialism, and poverty.

Key Points

- financial gain, success
- a new project
- lump sums if with appropriate cards

TWO OF PENTACLES
Card number 66

Traditional Points About the Card

A young man tries to balance two pentacles in an attempt to balance his financial affairs.

Modern Meaning

This is not a good card for money matters, because it means that the querent must pay attention to her bank account. Money will be short for a while and she will find herself juggling cash. Fortunately, the period of hardship is likely to be short-lived, so when you make this prediction be sure you give your client plenty of hope for the future. Twos in the tarot represent choices, and in this case, the querent will need to make decisions about money. Changing credit cards around for a better interest rate may help or getting cheaper mortgages and loans might be worthwhile.

This card also talks about writing letters and various kinds of communication.

R e v e r s e d

The querent will experience legal problems and holdups. There are broken promises in her future, but financial changes for the better are in the offing.

K e y   P o i n t s

- juggling money through tough times
- robbing Peter to pay Paul
- letters and communications
- decisions over cash

THREE OF PENTACLES
Card number 67

Traditional Points About the Card

A young person works hard to chisel away at the stone in order to make progress.

Modern Meaning

This card often signifies self-employment. Not everyone for whom you read will be freelance or have their own business, and not all will wish to do so. However, when this card appears, the querent is likely to be self-employed and supporting herself financially. If the querent is self-employed or wishes to become so, look at surrounding cards to decide upon the outcome. This is also the "apprenticeship card," so your querent may be learning new tasks or attending college or university.

Reversed

This card signifies family quarrels over money.

Key Points

- self-employment
- financial self-support
- college, university, or apprenticeships

FOUR OF PENTACLES
Card number 68

Traditional Points About the Card

A woman sits with four pentacles around her. Three are before her and one is above her. This shows the need to keep the majority of your money safe and spend only a little.

Modern Meaning

The querent must not overspend. Uncertain times may be on the way, so advise her to keep her cash safe. Alternatively, the querent could be around a person who has a preoccupation with money or someone who is stingy or miserly.

If this is next to a travel card, it could indicate failing a driving test.

Reversed

This card can mean a loss of money for the querent, or may signify that she is working hard for little reward.

Key Points

- do not overspend
- someone being mean or greedy with money
- a failed driving test if the Four of Pentacles appears with travel cards

FIVE OF PENTACLES
Card number 69

Traditional Points About the Card

Two miserable people sit comforting each other with five pentacles behind them. The blood-soaked bandages denote illness and hospitals. Many decks show the two figures out in the street with a lighted window behind them, suggesting that while others are warm, snug, healthy, and well fed—they are out in the cold.

Modern Meaning

This is a complicated card. When the Five of Pentacles is alone, it suggests worries and anxieties bombarding the querent, along with poor finances. With the Four of Wands, the Lovers, the Two of Cups, and the Ten of Cups, a separation or parting of a romantic relationship is likely. When the Five of Pentacles is with health cards, such as the Ten of Swords, the Devil, and the Four of Wands, it means that illness will engulf the querent or that someone close to her may need surgery or dental work. When it appears next to the Empress, a cesarean section is likely.

If more than one of the above cards appears with this five, it is best to use only one interpretation. For instance, if more relationship cards appear in the spread than health cards, consider a relationship breakdown. Alternatively, you may have a psychic inclination toward a particular card and its associated meaning.

Reversed

God is making the querent face a karmic lesson.

Key Points

- financial poverty
- operations and surgery
- separation within a relationship

SIX OF PENTACLES
Card number 70

Traditional Points About the Card

A man sits holding scales in one hand and handing out money with the other. He is weighing up his financial situation.

Modern Meaning

This card is reasonably good. Although there will not be any shortage of cash in the querent's future, she must still take care not to over-spend. The querent tends to be slightly overgenerous, perhaps spending too much on others. On a negative note, warn the querent against lending money or goods, as anything that she lends will be a long time coming back, if it ever does!

Reversed

Legal problems might occur. Someone may be buying a friendship. The querent must be careful not to throw good money after bad. Unpaid debts hang around.

Key Points

• spend some, save some
• no major problems with money
• never lend money because it may not come back
• the querent is being too generous

135

SEVEN OF PENTACLES
Card number 71

Traditional Points About the Card

A farmer stands ready to reap the benefits of his harvest. He looks toward the future and wonders whether God will bless his crop again.

Modern Meaning

The client might be worrying needlessly over money. Assure her that spirits will protect her. However, advise her not to take on any financial commitments within twelve months, as she could struggle to pay back loans.

If this card is next to a page, the querent might be around a very naughty child.

Reversed

The querent is waiting for change to occur. There may be broken promises over money.

Key Points

- needless concern over cash
- money gained through hard work
- warn against taking out loans
- around pages, this could relate to naughty children

EIGHT OF PENTACLES
Card number 72

Traditional Points About the Card

A man sits faithful to his project. The pentacles behind him are a symbol of his accomplishments. Two pentacles before him point toward continued efforts.

Modern Meaning

This is the card of study or coursework, and it shows an individual learning a new task. If you have established that the querent has children, her youngster may be taking exams or attending college or university. Look closely at the surrounding cards to determine success or failure. On the other hand, this could mean that the querent will take up further education or she may take courses relating to work.

Reversed

The querent could have trouble with her ego. She or someone near her may fail exams and courses.

Key Points

• course work, study, and exams
• new learning experiences

NINE OF PENTACLES
Card number 73

Traditional Points About the Card

Dressed lavishly, a woman wears pentacles around her neck, demonstrating her wealth.

Modern Meaning

This is a fabulous money card. Cash will come in, either in the form of a lump sum or in an ongoing way. There is no concern over finances. The spirit world will give the querent more than enough to live on. When this card is with the Ace of Pentacles, this suggests great wealth to come and it could even indicate a lottery win. However, the two cards would have to cross in the center of the spread on top of the significator card.

This card also denotes travel to exotic locations.

Reversed

The querent could be the victim of her own wealth. Money is good, but there is no love in the querent's life.

Key Points

- brilliant finances
- money coming in abundance
- lump sums and lottery wins

TEN OF PENTACLES
Card number 74

Traditional Points About the Card

A wealthy couple embrace. The pentacles near them demonstrate their financial security.

Modern Meaning

This relationship card concerns people who live together as a couple. Usually the pair will have struggled emotionally or financially in the past. However, their relationship is so strong that it can withstand the knocks in life. They will eventually enjoy financial rewards and have little or no worry over money. Such a relationship is so strong that even if the spread contains the Two of Swords, they will hear of someone else's divorce rather than having to face one of their own. If the Ten of Pentacles sits beside a group of Court cards, a family reunion or celebration is highly starred.

Reversed

The querent may experience problems with pensions and insurances. There may be taxation difficulties or legal and financial problems.

Key Points

- relationship or marriage card
- financial security
- the querent is able to take life's knocks
- family reunions

PAGE of PENTACLES.

PAGE OF PENTACLES
Card number 75

Traditional Points About the Card

A young person gazes at the countryside, taking in all there is to see. He holds one pentacle, a sign that his future will guarantee a life of financial security.

Modern Meaning

This child is mostly quiet and studious, the type who enjoys reading and learning. School will be important to him, so he will do his best to achieve high standards and good grades. This is the most intellectual of all the pages, so this youngster will have a good education and a good career to follow.

The coloring of this page is debatable. He could be blond or brown-haired and light eyed or dark eyed. Tradition suggests that the pentacle family is blond but as tarot has progressed, a modern approach has replaced this strict code.

As a Situation

There may be a small bonus, a small raise in salary, or a small windfall.

Reversed

The querent has bored, moody children with wasted talents near her.

Key Points

- a studious child who is interested in learning
- college or university later

KNIGHT OF PENTACLES

Card number 76

KNIGHT of PENTACLES.

Traditional Points About the Card

A proud knight holds himself in a stately fashion. The lance he holds is a phallic symbol and the pentacle in his hand represents his desire for financial gain.

Modern Meaning

This knight is a conscientious man who has worked and trained hard to achieve his goals. He is a clever, academic individual but he may not have reached his full potential, so there is still scope for him to further his education. In his teens, he will show little interest in women, owing to shyness, caution, or lack of sexual nerve. He will soon catch up, though, leaving all the other knights standing, and will go through a phase where he will be a real Romeo with many girlfriends. The difference between this knight and the others is that he will respect women and treat them well. In later years, he will be successful in business or his career and will be a high achiever.

As a Situation

Finances and business improve, but the querent will need to exercise caution. This card also represents journeys.

Reversed

This knight may be arrogant and unrealistic, so he needs to come back down to earth.

Key Points

- a clever and academic young man
- at first cautious in romance but he will catch up
- he will become a high achiever in business

QUEEN OF PENTACLES
Card number 77

Traditional Points About the Card

A queen bends forward on a pentacle; her clothes complement her beauty. The ripened fruit situated on the card symbolizes her maturity. She wears a large ring, to reveal continuity.

Modern Meaning

This woman has social graces; she is intellectual and elegant. Her interests lie in the arts; she is concerned with green issues and charity. She is usually an influential woman with a good business head on her shoulders. Her main fault is that she can be bossy, especially toward her children. Her thoughts run deep, making her hard to fathom.

As a Situation

There will be growth in business, career, or finances, or there will be money to spend on something important.

Reversed

This woman will marry for money. She is an interfering woman who gossips in society.

Key Points

- a beautiful woman who loves the arts and charities
- influential and inclined to be a bit bossy

KING of PENTACLES.

KING OF PENTACLES
Card number 78

Traditional Points About the Card

The king wears a helmet decorated with horns, suggesting a restless nature. He holds his scepter, which is a symbol of his authority.

Modern Meaning

This king is an attractive person who has established a certain position in life. He is in a position of authority and respect and is known for his efficiency and hard work. He started at the bottom of his career and worked his way up, but it is also possible that he inherited his position or his wealth. He may be a financial adviser or may work with figures and finances on a daily basis. He has a down-to-earth nature and a wonderful sense of humor. His parenting skills are good and he makes a very loving husband and father.

As a Situation

This card signifies success in business, finance, or property matters.

Reversed

This is a corrupt and perverse man who cannot be trusted.

Key Points

- a man of high standing
- respected at work and at home
- a kind, down-to-earth father

7

SPREADS

There are thousands of ways to lay out the tarot, but here a few that you can experiment with:

The Three, Three, Three, One Spread

Start at the top and read the first row of cards as a group. Then do the same with the second row and finally the third row. Then, take another card from the deck to represent the outcome. You will notice that this spread does not use a significator. If you wish, you can use one and place it directly above card number 2.

Final Outcome

The Sun Dial

This spread uses a significator. Place cards 1 and 2 facedown over the top of the significator. These cards predict what will be happening to the querent in the near future. Turn these over and then turn each of the other cards over one by one. This gives the querent a general twelve-month reading.

The Celtic Cross

The center six cards should relate to situations taking place at the time of the reading or in the near future. The four cards situated on the right should predict the future.

Group the cards together and read the suits as a whole. For instance, there may be three Cup cards suggesting a relationship matter, or a selection of Pentacles foretelling monetary issues.

You can link in any major arcana card with any minor arcana card to give the spread more impact.

The American Sundial

This spread requires a large space, so be sure to clear your table to make room for it.

Choose a card that you feel represents the querent and put it on the table. Then place the cards in the sequence shown in the diagram. The Sundial spread often gives a twelve-month forecast with each number depicting the month of the year. Turn each card over and then place three more cards on top of it from the shuffled pack.

149

8

TIPS AND TECHNIQUES

Whether you are only hoping to read for your friends and family or you hope to become a professional tarot reader, it is important to learn how to verbalize your predictions. A good approach at the onset of a reading is to tell the querent that the tarot cards show overall situations and that they do not always give dates and times. This means that the querent may not understand everything that is contained in the reading, but assure her that it will make sense later. Tell her to keep an open mind, because some of the things that appear in the cards may take six to twelve months or even longer to come about.

Many readers stick out their necks and try too hard. For example, saying to the querent, "I see you have a daughter," puts the reader in a vulnerable position. It is far better to be less definite and say something like, "The cards tell me that at some stage in your life you will have a little girl. Indeed, you may already have one." If the querent already has a daughter, she will usually say so. After this, you can examine the surrounding cards to establish whether they relate to this child or not. Sometimes the client will say that they have a son, so you can ask if the boy is sensitive, artistic, and gentle. Amazingly, this frequently turns out to be the case.

If you state categorically that your querent has just moved, she may reply that she has not and that she has no desire to do so, but if the cards are talking about a change of address, this is likely to happen some time later. The cards are rarely wrong, but if you make a mistake in your interpretation by being too confident, the client will go away thinking that you don't know your business. Perhaps suggest that the client will not always live in her current home, and say that the cards are pointing to a change of address. Say that this may have recently happened or that it seems to be on the horizon. Either way, the client will be impressed with your talent.

You can expect to get the timing wrong in a reading because the spirit world doesn't deal in time the way that we do on earth, but your reputation will be in tatters if you are too dogmatic and the client catches you out. Put everything in the future tense and you won't go wrong. For instance, "I can see a change of address here, but it may not have happened yet."

DON'T FISH

There is nothing worse than going to a tarot reader who asks endless questions. Never ask a direct question, because this is completely unprofessional.

Do not say, "Do you work?" "Are you married?" "Is your father dead?" The querent will not be impressed. This is fishing, and the readers who use this approach do not get many recommendations from their clients.

You can say, "You have lots of work-related cards in your spread: I take it you are working at the moment?" By telling the querent there are work cards, you are predicting the fact that she will be employed. The querent may tell you that she is not working at present, in which case you would go on to tell her that she will be working again in the near future.

You can say, "I can foresee a marriage or partnership for you." Nine times out of ten the querent will answer you by saying, "Yes, I'm married" or "I live with my boyfriend" or

"That would be nice." Any one of these answers will help you to predict future events with confidence. You can say, "You have a lovely man in the spirit world that is looking after you and watching over you." If the client's father is dead, she will usually say, "Could that be my dad?" or "Do you think that could be my grandfather?"

If her father is still alive and you ask her whether he is dead, she could start to believe that her father hasn't long to live. You have to be extremely careful in this instance, because most people who visit you will hang on to every word you say.

THE SAD CLIENT

Clients visit tarot readers because they have problems that make them vulnerable and unhappy. Your main aim is to guide these people and to lighten their load. Always bring about a positive outcome without making things up. In most cases, problematic situations do improve in time, and it is important that you make this clear. After hearing this, your client will often start to take a positive attitude. Not everyone has solid friendships and family at hand, so help and constructive advice may be just what the client needs. As a reader you will often be asked for your opinion, but be cautious and think before you speak. You will have a profound influence on your client and on her future actions.

When you have been reading for a while, you will almost certainly come across the occasional client who is suicidal. This incredibly difficult situation puts you in a very responsible position. In these circumstances, tell the querent that God never gives us anything that we cannot cope with and that our purpose on earth is to learn and develop spiritually, and we do this by living through difficult times. Tell the client that if she chooses to end her life, she will have to come back down and do it all over again. Whether this is true or not is debatable, but it might prevent the client from doing something foolish while she is in the throes of her problems. Depending in which country you live, you can also suggest that if she feels particularly vulnerable in the middle of the night that she should contact in the United States 1-800-SUICIDE (1-800-784-2433) or the Samaritans in the United Kingdom (08457 90 90 90).

Tell an unhappy client that the spirit will bless her (especially if she prays for strength) and that she is not on her own. Then bring about some positive aspects to the reading and predict future events with enthusiasm. Try to show her that there is a much sunnier future waiting out there for her once she has lived through this awful time. Be sympathetic.

Throughout my time as a reader, the majority of suicidal clients were young men between the ages of twenty and thirty. They were usually at rock bottom because of either women or drugs. You can give help and gentle advice. Over time, you will see yourself not as a tarot reader but as more of a psychic counselor.

THE SILENT CLIENT

The silent client is quite frustrating and common. A person will arrive for a reading and will sit stony-faced throughout. Once you have established that the client wants you to conduct the entire reading without her opening up, there is little that you can do. Put everything in the future tense and try not to let the client get to you. If you are really struggling, tell the querent that she has a force field around her, and that if she doesn't relax you cannot proceed. Another good approach is to ask the client whether she feels that you have predicted something that has already happened. This usually breaks the ice. The chances are that once you make one or two "direct hits," then she will relax.

THE MOTORMOUTH CLIENT

The motormouth client is actually much worse than the silent client. A number of people sit and talk all the way through a reading. If you give this client a tape of the reading, all she will hear is her own voice on it because you won't have been able to get a word in edgewise.

You may mention something about her husband, and she will go on to tell you all about his job, his ex-wife, and his bad back. In fact, she will tell you all the things that you can clearly see in the reading and that you were just about to say. These readings can last for ages, and when the job is done, you will feel dreadful because you will consider that you have not predicted anything. These people obviously love company and like to chat. It might be the only reason they have booked an appointment to see you in the first place. You may feel like telling them to shut up, but it's best to let them rattle on.

THE OBSTINATE CLIENT

About one in every ten people you see will be pigheaded, rude, and disrespectful. Why she bothers to visit a psychic is beyond me! She normally comes in with an attitude and takes great pleasure in watching you squirm. I won't have any of this nonsense and neither should you. The typical scenario is to disagree or laugh at everything you say, or to shake her head every time you make a future prediction. Always remain calm and never lose your temper. Your blood may be boiling, but be professional and hide your emotions.

You can battle on, regardless, with the reading and then take her money. You worked hard enough for it, so you deserve it. Alternatively, you can say that you feel she is on a negative vibration and that you cannot possibly conduct a reading for her. The obstinate client hates this, so she will usually start to behave. If you do send the client away without a reading, never charge her. In most cases, she nearly always tries to book an appointment with you again, but this time with an open mind.

SHOULD I CHARGE FOR MY READINGS?

The simple answer to this is yes. This is a regularly disputed matter, but you have to remember that if you do not charge a fee for your readings, you will work very hard all day and every day from the goodness of your heart. This will prevent you from being able to find alternative employment and leave you drained and exhausted without any reward for your efforts.

Being psychic is a gift. Over time, you will do your fair share of free readings, so charging a small fee for your time is not asking too much. Find out what the local going rate is and then offer your readings at a similar or slightly lower price. As you become more experienced, you can charge more.

INDEX